James and the Books

by Brooke Dugan
illustrated by Chris Vallo

Practice Decodable 89

McGraw Hill Education

Bothell, WA • Chicago, IL • Columbus, OH • New York, NY

MHEonline.com

McGraw-Hill Education

Send all inquiries to:
McGraw-Hill Education
8787 Orion Place
Columbus, OH 43240-4027

ISBN: 978-0-02-145137-1
MHID: 0-02-145137-0

Printed in China.

8 9 10 11 12 DSS 27 26 25 24 23

"Let's talk about good books," said Miss Smith.
"This is about humans landing on the moon."

James did not like books too much. But going to the moon would be cool. He might like that book.

Emma stood up. "This book is about a cute, little goose that got lost," she said.

James would not like a goose book! But he asked, "Did big geese find the little goose?"

Emma said yes. James was glad.

"I read about a football team. Fans thought the team would not win, but the team did!" Tom said.

"Wow!" said James.

Nicole said, "My dad fixes trucks. He uses a book to help him. He said it is his best tool! That book must be good!"

James shook his head up and down. A good book could help! James made up his mind. He would choose good books to read, too!

Miss Smith's room had a book nook. James took a book about cooking. He read it fast. It was good.

James took a book about wooden boats. He read it. He would like to see those boats.

Then James read a book about kangaroos. Kangaroos were cool! James looked for more good books.

That afternoon, James read a book about strange foods. Then he read a book called *Chip, the Choo Choo*. Next, he read about big balloons.

James read about a boy with a bug zoo. He read about how swimming pools are made. James took three more books home.

That night, James found the book he liked the most. It was about Robin Hood, a brave man from long ago.

The next day James said, "This is a fantastic book! I read it over and over."

Miss Smith said, "James, you read ten books! You like books!"

James did!